Commodities Trading For Beginners: How To Make Money With Commodities Trading

Russell Ingram

Table of contents

Introduction

Chapter 1: What are Commodities?

Chapter 2: History of Trading Commodity Futures

Chapter 3: Commodities as an Investment Vehicle

Chapter 4: Risk Trading Commodity Futures

Chapter 5: Proper Way to Trade Commodities

Chapter 6: Developing a Good Commodities Trading Plan

Chapter 7: Real World Aspects – Applying Your Knowledge in Commodity Futures

Chapter 8: A Final Chapter Insert on Bitcoin and Virtual Currencies, and Some Risks Involved

© **Copyright 2015 - All rights reserved.**

This document is geared towards providing exact and reliable information in regards to the topic and issue covered. The publication is sold with the idea that the publisher is not required to render accounting, officially permitted, or otherwise, qualified services. If advice is necessary, legal or professional, a practiced individual in the profession should be ordered.

- From a Declaration of Principles which was accepted and approved equally by a Committee of the American Bar Association and a Committee of Publishers and Associations.

In no way is it legal to reproduce, duplicate, or transmit any part of this document in either electronic means or in printed format. Recording of this publication is strictly prohibited and any storage of this document is not allowed unless with written permission from the publisher. All rights reserved.

The information provided herein is stated to be truthful and consistent, in that any liability, in terms of inattention or otherwise, by any usage or abuse of any policies, processes, or directions contained within is the solitary and utter responsibility of the recipient reader. Under no circumstances will any legal responsibility or blame be held against the publisher for any reparation, damages, or monetary loss due to the information herein, either directly or indirectly.

Respective authors own all copyrights not held by the publisher.

The information herein is offered for informational purposes solely, and is universal as so. The presentation of the information is without contract or any type of guarantee assurance.

The trademarks that are used are without any consent, and the publication of the trademark is without permission or backing by the trademark owner. All trademarks and brands within this book are for clarifying purposes only and are the owned by the owners themselves, not affiliated with this document.

Introduction

I want to thank you and congratulate you for purchasing the book, *"Commodities Trading for Beginners: How to Make Money with Commodities Trading"*.

I created this book as an introduction to the world of commodities and futures markets. There are a total of seven chapters and as you read from the beginning to the end, you'll get a better understanding of the market and how you can utilize these points towards your own personal trading strategy.

The first few chapters will take you on a historic trip back towards the origin of the commodities market. There are many definitions and points made on how the past commodity exchanges formed the modern version that we use currently. You will also learn what the true definition of a commodity is.

Unlike the other investment vehicles, the commodities futures market has inherent risks that you should be aware of before fully investing your money into any broker or platform. Together with the list of risks, there are many suggestions that professional commodity traders use each day to overcome these downfalls.

You will also find an easy, step-by-step guide on how you can develop a proper way of trading commodities. Each step will broaden your horizon on what it takes to start trading commodities and slowly lead yourself to possibly become a successful trader, similar to the 5% that are professionals in this game.

As you continue to read throughout the rest of the chapters, you'll develop a more enriched knowledge on trading this security and all the risks that you are exposed to. This book was not created as a textbook, but rather as a letter from a mentor to a student. Each point and subject has been tailored to answer your questions as you progressively continue to read the material.

Please take your time reading each chapter. If you rush through it, you may miss some points that are crucial to your growth as a commodities investor.

I wish you best of luck in your path towards succeeding in the commodities market.

Thanks again for purchasing this book, I hope you enjoy it!

Chapter 1: What are Commodities?

It's a very simple question. If I were to ask you this question, the most probable answer that you'd reply with would be "gold" or the more infamous "oil". Although these answers are excellent examples, they don't quite elaborate on what commodities *really* are. Once you understand a commodity truly is, you'll be on your way to become a more educated commodity trader.

Commodities are physical objects that originate from the earth such as milk, orange juice, cattle, crops, silver, gold and oil. There are many other commodities that are exchanged in different countries across the globe, but the main aspect of this market is that people purchase and sell these "assets" based on speculation.

Let's take a closer look at the commodity Orange Juice. Believe it or not, this is one of the first places that many commodity investors trace their beginnings from. It all began from an old movie called "Trading Places" in 1983 that portrayed Eddy Murphy ad Aykroyd who tried to strike it rich by making false information about frozen concentrated orange juice in order to change the market on his commodity.

You might be asking *"How could they strike it rich from frozen OJ that costs only $1.84 at Walmart? They must be crazy thinking that people trade OJ in Wall Street."*

Well just to let you know, orange juice is traded with a monetary volume that is in the billions Frozen concentrated orange juice (FCOJ) isn't really exchanged in the way that the film had depicted, but it is still true that a lot of money is traded in a short amount of time.

Fungibility

The definition of fungibility is an asset's ability to interchange with other assets of the same type. For example, certain grades of commodities, such as No. 3 or 5 orange juices are fungible because, well, they're simply orange juice. No matter where they are grown, there isn't much of a difference between the orange juices from the oranges that grow in your backyard compared to an orchard in a Midwest farm. They all end up in the same bottle that you drink during meals.

As long as the orange juice meets the standards i.e. ripeness, comes from a well-treated farm, taste is reasonable, etc., the juice that you drink is the same as the juice that I drink.

A second example of a commodity that has exhibits fungibility is Gold. Gold that is in Australia is the exact same gold that is in London, in respect to the purity level.

Fungibility is the first characteristic that defines a commodity. This quality allows you to trade large volumes of commodities such as gold, oil, natural gas and orange juice with only one price. No one can make a strong distinction between my gold and your gold; it's just gold and it's sold for XX amount of money per ton.

External Factors with Commodities

Fungibility is one of the very essences of what defines a commodity. Commodities are also great investments that are driven based on the external factors such as weather. If there is a hurricane that went over South America and destroyed crops such as coffee, then you as a commodity investor would purchase as much of the crop as you can. This way, if you are correct in your judgment, the price of the coffee crop would rise significantly because the surviving crops would be worth more due to the low supply and high demand.

Liquidity

Having liquidity is very critical for commodities trading. Each commodity is exchanged in markets that consist of active buyers and sellers who are constantly trading with one another. Having liquidity gives you as a commodity investor the option to enter and exit out of an investment without the need to find a buyer or seller that is willing to purchase or sell your commodities.

Commodities consist of speculators who add on to the market by providing the liquidity and assume the price fluctuation risk. They are able to earn a significant amount of profits from this method. This method of trading this market has existed for years. Now that you have a surface concept on what commodities are, let's take a look at the history behind this market.

Chapter 2: History of Trading Commodity Futures

History of Trading

Commodities Futures has existed for many years. The first time that this type of trading was recorded was with rice in the 17th century in Japan. Despite this knowledge, there's also some proof that there may have been rice futures that were exchanged in China 6000 years ago.

Commodities futures stems from the natural outgrowth of issue of global issues in maintaining an annual supply of seasonal products, such as agricultural crops. In the country of Japan, the merchants would use large warehouses to store rice for future use. The merchants had to find a solution to earn money. In order to do solve this dilemma, warehouse holders would sell receipts against the rice that was stored. These receipts were known as "rice tickets". Later on, the rice tickets were accepted by the general public as an alternate currency for commercial trading.

Multiple historians have also traced rice trading occurring in the Amsterdam during the late 1600s. Soon the Dojima rice market from Japan began to expand to multiple investors across the globe, which has been credited as the foundation of the future trading that still holds today in the modern commodities futures exchange.

Around 1840, the invention of the telegraph and the steamship were two great milestones in the commodities futures exchange history. They revolutionized the process of price formation in the futures exchange market. After the creation of these two inventions, supply and demand that were not local were placed into the trading market. The steamship helped reduce the time that it took to ship items from one country to another. What took two months to receive could take only a few weeks. Steam shipping was rather expensive, and what came about instead was the reliance on the most valuable thing, information.

At the end of the 1800s, there were five major commodity exchanges in the global business: New York, Liverpool, Alexandria, New Orleans and Havre. They were all connected via the transatlantic cable. If there was an adverse event that happened in once city, it would affect the others respectively.

Not all was peaches and cream in the world of commodities exchange. During WWII, most exchanges began to slow down and collapse. They began to lose their significance due to the country's priority being diverted towards the war. During the post war period, many governments sought to intervene with the commodities markets, specifically the agricultural securities. They set many rules to prohibit commodities trading. To assure that the rule was enforced, some countries with strong state control such as India, Egypt and China used stock holding systems that further crippled the markets.

It wasn't until the 1970s when the exchanges began to be rejuvenated. After Bretton Woods system had collapsed, multiple markets began to arise anew. Many interest rate markets and exchange rates were introduced. The dollar was not tied to the gold commodity anymore and oil soon had its own market.

Moving forward to the modern era, financial futures were introduced that brought higher stakes for investors in the market. The United States decided to create a method of regulation by forming the Commodity Futures Trading Commission which oversaw the futures market.

The commodities futures exchange didn't quite begin with a perfect structure. It took time and errors to create the market that we now use in the present day. Now that you understand the origins of the commodities exchange, let's take a look at how this financial instrument is used as an investment vehicle.

Chapter 3: Commodities as an Investment Vehicle

Commodity trading has some advantages as an investment vehicle that other alternative methods of investments don't have i.e. savings accounts, options, stock trading, and bonds. The main component of commodities trading is that there is a high potential to gain large profits within a short time period. If you've traded foreign exchange currencies, then you understand how leverage has a part in how this type of feat is feasible.

In the financial market, having a leverage means that you use borrowed capital to make your investments, with the expectation of earning higher amounts of profits from it. In other words, you can have a small amount of capital and buy a commodities futures contract that could be worth 10x as much as your initial pay. Similar to a double-edged sword, the leverage can either help you or hurt you. A small price change in the futures market could either produce large masses of profits for your account or lead to painful losses and possibly bankruptcy.

Trading in the commodities futures market has been shown to have the highest leverage than any other investment due to the initial margins that are established by the exchanges. These margins are very small compared to the contracts that are placed. This is an aspect of the futures market that is very useful but simultaneously being highly risky. If you have a small margin relative to the cash value of each commodities futures contract, the higher your leverage will be.

For example, if you as a commodities futures investor have $15,000 in your trading account and would like to purchase a long position in a contract for an index that is currently at 1300. The contract's value is only worth $350 times the specified index ($350 * 1300 = $455,000). This means that every point that is gained or lost in the index, you will gain or lose $250.

Within 6 months' time, you find that the index gained a total of 6.5%. This means that the index increased by 84.5 points to equal 1385 (rounded number). As for the money aspect, you as a commodity futures investor will have gained a return of $21,125 (84.5 points * $250). That's a 141% return from your investment.

Looking at the other angle, if the index decreased by 6.5%, then you would have lose $21,125 – a large amount of money compared to the capital that you deposited for the contract. I assume you've realized that there's still an amount left after your account has been depleted. This amount, $6,125 will still need to be paid from you. The fact that such a small percentage can result in a large profit or a detrimental loss is the risk factor that comes with leverage.

The tremendous amount of returns that is potentially possible within a short time period, despite the risk, is what attracts investors into this market. This is the first advantage that the commodities futures market has over the other financial investment vehicles.

The second advantage that commodities futures have as an investment vehicle is the low commissions. The commission that you are required to pay for the $21,125 profit would have been within the range of $40 to $60. The commissions that need to be paid from individual stocks that are purchased are close to one percent for both purchases and sales. You would have paid thousands of dollars simply to buy and sell a batch of stocks.

Another factor that is evident when trading commodities is that not every decision is always correct. In fact, it is very difficult to consistently make the correct decisions on what to buy and sell. Speculating in commodities offers to you an important advantage over other non-liquid investment vehicles i.e. real estate. The total balance that you have in your trading account is always available for you whenever you need it. As long as you maintain a certain margin, you are more than able to spend your profits that you've earned on an open trade without closing the position. Other investment vehicles such as stocks and bonds, you can't withdraw your profits until the asset has been sold.

We're going to go even further learning about commodity trading in this book, and as you continue to learn the full background of commodities future trading, you'll soon realize that the trading process is not as complex as it's made out to be. The commodities market only consists of around forty futures markets that you can trade in. Other markets such as the Stock exchange, there are thousands of potential assets that are available to trade. They cover many areas and sectors of the world economy.

As an investment vehicle, commodities trading give you the ability of making profits whether the future increases or decreases in value. Having a diversified portfolio of the futures markets allows you to take advantage of any economic scenario that is evident. Whether there economy is in a depression or is booming, droughts, famines, war, or harsh winters, there's always an opportunity that is presented to you when trading commodities.

With futures trading, there are some tax advantages that are offered to you as a commodities trader. Regardless of how long the holding period is, the profits that you make trading commodities are automatically taxed at a percentage of 60% in the long term gains and 40% in the short term gains. The highest rate that is taxed on your profits is 33%, which is a lot less than the highest rate for the average individual's income. If by chance there will be a re-establishment so that the taxation rates on the long term profits are lower than the profits on the short term positions, commodity traders will surely benefit from this.

Trading in the commodities futures market is an excellent investment vehicle. The advantages that it has to offer, despite the risks, give investors all the benefits and possibility of earning thousands of dollars in profits. Before we look into how a trade is placed, let's take an in-depth look at the risks that are inherent in commodities futures trading.

Chapter 4: Risk Trading Commodity Futures

You shouldn't get too excited, now that you've learned all about the large profits that are possible when trading commodity futures. It's essential to have a realistic approach when looking at how you trade with this, and any other investment vehicle. There will be times when you will have losses. There aren't any strategies that will give you 100% winning trades each time. Even professionals that trade this market for a living keep a reality check when the make each trade. They understand that the risk of losing a trade is much higher than actually winning.

We've read on how leverage carries a risk for commodity future traders. The possibility of losing more money than what you invested is more than enough to make an individual cringe and stay away from any type of investments. In fact, it is very understandable for a novice trader to refrain from trading risky investments ever again after attempting to trade commodities.

What is it about commodity futures trading that make it more risky than any other type of investments?

Unlike the stock market and other trading vehicles where you are limited in the amount of loss based on your investment, commodity futures trading leaves you exposed to a liability that is nearly unlimited. This limitless trading system can cause go beyond the amount that you have in your commodity futures trading account. The leverage attribute that we touched base with earlier is what gives this market its infamous reputation. As a matter of fact, there have been multiple futures traders that went bankrupt and owed a lot of money simply from trading this market in a short time period.

Let's take a look at a list of the risks that you are exposed to when trading commodity futures.

Unlimited Liability

When it comes to trading futures, one of the main facts that you have to face is that you will have unlimited liability exposed to your account. What this means is that you have the possibility of accruing losses that are far beyond your investment capital. As long as the price of the asset that's been chosen continues to progress in either direction, the amount of losses that you have from your trading positions will continuously accumulate.

Unlike option trading where you only lose the amount of money invested in each trade, trading in the commodities futures market, you have to account for a small percentage of the position value that you've made which is known as the "initial margin". This is necessary for you to place a commodity futures position.

If you do suffer any types of losses, they will get deducted from your initial margin. Afterwards a margin call is made when the initial margin is too low. If the loss is large enough to wipe out your initial margin that you deposited and you don't have enough funds to cover for the losses made, then you will be required to pay money to the broker and possibly lead you to bankruptcy if you can't be able to pay it off.

Having an unlimited liability can be managed by utilizing strict rules in trade placement as well as practicing sound risk management in the commodity futures market. These two key factors are what newbie traders in the commodity futures market have that makes it highly risky for them.

Leverage

Having leverage in the market is tied very closely to the unlimited liability that we discussed before. Depending on the initial margin ratio, commodities futures trading could give you leverage anywhere from 5 to 100 times. This characteristic is excellent when it comes to prices that are moving in the direction that you predicted in your analysis. However, it is a double edged sword that has the possibility of harming you back. If the price were to move against you, then your trading positions would be moving towards leveraged losses.

Let's look at an example of this scenario. You've performed your fundamental and analytical analysis and you've come to the conclusion on a direction of the market. You take notice that only $20 is needed for your initial margin on an asset that is valued at $200. Despite the intricate calculations and strategy that you implemented, the asset takes a turn for the worse and decreases by $20. At this point you have instantly made a 100% loss on your initial margin and the price of the underlying asset has lowered by a mere 10%. This is how leverage carries a risk in the commodities futures market and can make it nearly impossible for any type of futures trader to commit all of their eggs into one futures trading position.

Positioning sizing is very important when trading commodities because controls the dollar values that are being invested in each trade.

Geopolitical Risk

This is one of the inherent risks is that associated with trading commodities. The risk is that most of the world's natural resources are located in multiple continents and there are different jurisdictions that are placed by the foreign governments, companies and other independent entities. For example, most of the oil that many nations need in their economy is found in abundance in the Persian Gulf region. Most oil companies have to negotiate with these countries in the Middle East for access to their oil supply.

These types of negotiations can get quite intense and lead to disagreements that have the probability of affecting a whole nation's economic welfare. These disagreements involve taxes, concern for the environment, licensing agreements and many other issues that are complex in nature.

A Country that has a strong control over a commodity that multiple nations require can simply kick out companies that they see are not beneficial to them. Unfortunately there isn't a magic formula that you can use to completely protect yourself from this risk. The most efficient way of minimizing this risk exposure is to invest in companies that have economies and experience of a large scale. Companies that have a long track record in dealing with geopolitical risk will help manage this risk for you. A small company that is still an infant in the market won't have this sort of experience and may face even more risk than the former. In the commodities market, this is a key factor to always consider.

Speculative Risk

In the commodities market, there are many investors who are primarily interested in earning quick profits in the short term by speculation on a commodities price direction. This is a risk in that they can cause the markets to move in many different ways. Even though the speculators provide the liquidity that is beneficial to all traders, they are capable of causing the market to be highly volatile. Because these speculators can lose control in this area, similar to the housing bubble and the dot.com phenomenon, you should always be cautious about how much speculation is evident in the commodities market.

When there are too much speculative funds that are being introduced into the commodities futures market, there can be some detrimental effects that may happen. If you spot that there is an unusual activity of speculation, the best idea would be to avoid trading in the markets for a time. Only until the volatility has subsided is when you can re-enter the markets.

Fraudulent Activities

If feels like there's just too many factors that bring high risk to you as a commodities investor. To add on to the extensive list is the possibility of fraudulent activity. Even though the Commodity Futures Trading Commission has been set to regulate the exchange activities in the market, there's still a possibility that you may become a fraud victim.

Researching the firms that you invest your hard earned money in is one way to prevent yourself from being a victim of this risk. There are times when no extensive amount of research or discipline can protect you from fraudulent activities. This is a simple fact of the game. You simply have to take this into account with a grain of salt.

The SEC administers and enforces the federal laws that govern the sale and trading of securities, such as stocks, bonds, and mutual funds, but they do not regulate futures trading.

With limited exceptions, the trading of futures must be executed on the floor of a commodity exchange. Similar to broker-dealers that are members of the Financial Industry Regulatory Authority, or some other self-regulatory organization, all firms and individuals who trade futures with the public or give advice about futures trading must be registered with the National Futures Association (NFA).

The CFTC cautions investors to be wary of websites that purport to offer high yield investment opportunities in futures and options, forex, hedge fund, or precious metals, common areas of internet fraud. The CFTC has posted several fictitious websites that are representative of typical websites that have been the subject of CFTC enforcement actions. These examples include some of the hallmarks of commodity futures fraud. CFTC's examples of fraudulent websites include: Global Financial Capital Management, Colfax Trading International, TradeForex4You, White, Truman and Fischer, Excalibier Precious Metals, and Commodity Profits.com. They are definitely worth checking out.

Chapter 5: Proper Way to Trade Commodities

Now that you have a good understanding on how the commodities market works and the risks that you are at risk of being exposed to, we can begin the process towards actually trading the market. The first step towards trading the commodities market is education. I'm not talking about education on the history of the market. I'm talking about training education; knowledge that you obtain that will come in handy once you begin executing trade positions with your real money.

A great step towards achieving this step is to find a trader that has been successful in the market themselves. Nothing compares to the amount of wisdom that you will receive from them since they encompass your final goal. They can personally coach you and teach you on how they trade the market. If you do get the chance to find a trader who has the time and patience to educate you, don't waste that opportunity. That is the perfect chance for you to soak in as much knowledge that you can from them. By doing so, you'll be able to avoid the multiple mistakes that you may make in your path towards being a successful commodities trader.

You should also take into account that finding the proper way to trade is a combination of what you've learned and from experience that you've gained. Just because one method works for your mentor doesn't necessarily mean that it will work for you as well. You may not have the capital or years of experience that is necessary to trade in the way that the professionals trade. Taking small characteristics from the knowledge that you've gained from your mentors and developing your own personal style of trading will lead you progressively towards being a successful commodities trader.

Demo Trading

Another way of developing the proper way of trading commodities is to use trial and error. Using a demo trading account is the best choice that most beginners use because you have the option of practicing any style and strategy that you want without worrying about depleting your account with real money. It's a great method on its own, but you should also consider random reinforcement. This means that you could practice trading on a demo account, get really lucky and generate tons of profits by trading idiotically. Or you could accumulate multiple losses with the use of an effective system. This is one of the downfalls to utilizing trial and error in demo trading.

"But aren't you contradicting yourself? I thought that demo trading was an excellent idea?"

I'm not contradicting myself, but rather informing you in a realistic approach. This way you don't fall for this pitfall that many beginners end up in a short period of time.

In order to counter random reinforcement is to read books. Using your local library, online websites and any other sources that are written by credible and well respected authors will help you overcome this downfall in trial and errors. Yet similar to demo trading, reading books also has its own pitfall. A secret that is truly evident, yet subtly shown in commodity trading, is that most of the materials that you learn from books rarely work in the real world.

"What do you mean?"

Even though many books from these well respected authors have trading strategies that seem effective, they will more than likely lose money when they are implemented in a live market environment. It's shocking to find out, but most commodity future authors show the effectiveness that their trading strategies have. The best option for you is to take some of the examples and sample each one to see how effective they are in different market scenarios.

"So what should I do to ACTUALLY trade properly?"

You should learn to combine all the ideas and knowledge that you've accumulated together with the practical experience that you have achieved by watching the live market. Learning to trade properly doesn't take one full week to obtain. It takes a lot of time and diligence. You should set a time each day and take note of all the mistakes that you've seen and further improve your approach continuously. By doing this, you're gaining priceless experience and knowledge that you can't get from a book or anyone else.

Of course intelligence and practice isn't the only qualities of what it takes to trade properly. You should also have a good control of your emotions, self-awareness of what your trading style is, and discipline. Applying these parts is detrimental towards guiding you towards success in trading commodities. You should also remember that you don't need to have some space scientific strategy that only an astrophysicist can understand and apply.

Try to use Occam's razor. This means that you shouldn't use the most complex system, but rather the simplest approach that is simultaneously effective in trading commodities. Most trading plans that are successful tend to be simple. They utilize Occam's razor's principle of comprising all of the main principles of proper trading in a unique, yet simple way.

Chapter 6: Developing a Good Commodities Trading Plan

In chapter seven of this book, we'll be looking at seven steps that you can take to develop your own unique strategy towards becoming a successful commodities futures trader. This shouldn't take you more than seven days to fully understand. Within seven hours you should get a good grasp on how to trade commodities with these seven steps.

(The multiple occurrence of the word "seven" was just a word-play to bring some humor to your reading. Don't fall asleep yet. You're almost done with the book!)

Step One: The Starting Line

In every business plan, the first step that is made is to create a plan. Every professional trader always formulates a trading plan with the total amount of capital that they are capable of investing. Before you deposit any amount of money into a broker, you should first understand that in this type of market, being successful is directly related with the amount that you invest in your capital. The more funds you place in your investments, the higher the probability that you will make more money.

You should also ask yourself the question, *"What is the minimum amount that you should begin trading with?"*

The average amount that most expert professionals recommend to begin with is $10,000. The reason why isn't because this is the magic number. Rather, to be able to stay afloat and survive for a longer period in this type of exchange market, you need a substantial amount that you can use to create larger profits and cover the many losses that you may experience. Also your success in any trade that you place with an investment that is lower than this number will most likely be based on luck. In order to practice proper risk management principles, you need a large enough capital to work with.

An important thing to remember is that the money that you will be investing in your capital will be "at risk". You shouldn't consider investing money that you will need to pay your monthly expenses. This should be money that you can afford to lose without having any effect on your everyday life.

Think of your commodities trading account as a business. It's a fact that there are many businesses that do fail. This is the simple fact of life. You should have a strong mindset when it comes to trading in this market. Having the stomach to accept the losses without fear and hindering your capability of making the right trading decisions is very important to you as a commodity futures investor.

Step 2: The markets that you'll trade.

The second step you should take when creating your commodities trading plan is to know what securities that you'll be trading with in the market. There are around 40 futures markets that have enough liquidity to allow some strict speculation. For more protection against high risk, the rule of thumb is to find the market that fits to your risk level, trading method and the size of your account.

Once you've decided on a market that suits your preference, consider diversifying your portfolio. There are many large price movements that happen each year in a market, but it is unknown on what date and time that they will happen in advance. Diversifying will give you a higher probability of catching a few of these opportunities that account for being successful in trading commodities.

Looking at the historical data of each market will further assist you in deciding what markets tend to have large trending movements. The trend will always be your friend until it ends, but before that occurs, you want to maximize the advantage that it has to offer by choosing the markets that are more likely to trend.

There are four different sectors in the commodities and in each one there are certain securities that are the most chosen among many investors. Here's a list of them:

- Energy: Crude Oil, Natural Gas and Heating Oil are the most excellent choices in this sector.

- Food: Orange Juice, Coffee and Sugar are the most highly selected.

- Metals: Silver, Gold, Copper.

- Agriculture: Soybeans, Cotton, Oats and Corn.

Now that you know to some degree what markets you would like to trade in, you can continue forward in understanding how fundamental and technical analysis come into play in deciding your trade positions.

Step 3: Technical Analysis & Fundamental Analysis

These two terms are a reference to the two methods that investors use to analyze and forecast the future trend growth of stocks and other assets. Similar to any other investment strategy, they each have their own promoters and challengers.

Fundamental: This method is used by investors to perform an attempted measurement of the intrinsic value of an asset. This analysis methodology is used to achieve a study of the whole picture; the industrial conditions, the economic welfare and even the management of the specific companies.

Technical: This is the analytical method that studies the securities by using statistics that are generated by the activity in the markets i.e. historical volume and price trends. Technical analysts don't try to measure the intrinsic value of a security, but instead use charts to find the trends and patterns that may give a suggestion towards the probable price movements.

Both of these methods have their advantages against the other, but in reality, neither is better than the other. When trading commodities, we lean more towards the technical analysis. Not because it's been deemed superior in this market, but rather it's a great way to start trading as a beginner because it's a lot easier than analyzing fundamentally. Once you become more comfortable with technical analysis, you can move on towards the fundamental analysis where you will study the interaction of supply and demand and how it affects the price of the commodity market.

One of the main principles of technical analysis is that history tends to repeat itself. This means that there are certain patterns that re-occurred in the past that are identifiable and can be used to foreshadow possible directions that the price movements may make in the future. These chart patterns that you will observe on the commodity charts will provide you with the tools that you need to forecast the price movements in the near future. There are some chart patterns that are reliable and some that aren't.

These chart patterns are not unfailing. The all have the probability of providing successful trades. They just don't give you a full guarantee that they will work 100% of the time. You as a trader must stay alert on any possible chart signs that may show that your analysis is incorrect. By using support and resistance lines, you can further increase the accuracy of your analysis, entry and exit of your trades in the market.

In order to become a better chart analyst, you should study further on different technical analysis methods, how to use the support & resistance levels to measure the price action, how to identify trends and how technical indicators further increase the precision and accuracy of your trades. The more you understand these concepts, the further away that the illusion of the market's randomness will progressively disappear.

In order to find charts to analyze the commodity market, simply make a Google search for "commodity charts" and you'll find different websites that offer charts to you for any commodity that you require.

Step 4: The Trend is Your Friend

This next step is part of the 3rd step, but deserves its own step because of how effective it is towards your trading strategy. Trading with the trend offers you larger potential profits in the long term because you are following the true direction that the market is headed towards instead of making prediction on where it would possibly go towards.

There are many times where you'll spot a trend but will feel as though your entry was too late in the trend and you may have possibly missed the ride. The best way to be confident that your entry was correct is to look at a particular time frame. For example, if you're identifying a trend, it should be a daily, two-week or monthly time frame. By adhering to a specific time frame, you'll be more assured in your decision making.

Trends do occur in all the time frames, but the time frames that have produced better results time and time again stem from the longer term periods. The longer you hold on to a trading position, the large the profits you will gain. The trends that last for months are more stable compared to the short term time frames. As long as you use your money management and correct judgment from your chart analysis, you should be able to lock in more successful profits consistently in the long term.

Step 5: Cut your losses short

Following the trend is one aspect of trading commodities that will bring you profits. But the question that arises is *"when is the right time to exit your trades if they aren't any profits being earned?"*

As a trader, you would like to have a profit before you close any open trade positions. But more importantly, you don't want to lose any of your money. It's very hard to stop a trade because it hits your ego. It's very hard to admit that you were wrong in the trading decision that you made. This is a characteristic that many professional traders have learned to overcome in order to be successful in this market. They accept that there will be losses in this game. They understand that the markets are very random and that even the most polished trading strategies will have a few losses. Having a couple of losses to them doesn't destroy their ego with the thought that they were wrong.

Adopting their attitude towards losses will help you as well to see that being wrong a couple of times doesn't mean the end of the world. The best way to continue to profit is to make the losses miniscule in comparison to the total investment account. If you want to continue your career as a commodity trader, you need to maintain your trading capital from depleting. Trading in the direction of the overall trend will help you make large profits. As long as you don't make large losses, your capital will continue to survive and you will continue to enjoy the large profits that you make.

Understanding the laws of probability will help you realize that no matter which method you take in trading in the market, you will most certainly receive a few losses along the way. If you were to place a large amount of money from your capital in all of your trades, one of those losses will most definitely hurt your account size.

There are many other complex ways of exiting a trade and cutting your losses short, but no matter what your situation may be, getting yourself out of the market after receiving a loss of a significant amount of money will help you the same way as any other. The important part is that you use good stop losses, and money management to limit the losses that you face and have a way to compensate for them in the future trades.

Step 6: Let your profits run

This step correlates with the fourth step. If you notice that you have an excellent trade that is accumulating a good amount of profits from a strong trend, you can continue to take advantage of the trend while earning money for your account. You should utilize these opportunities for as long as you can because the strong trend may last for even more days, weeks or even months.

We discussed that there are some risks that can happen if you were to ride the trend for too long. A method that professional investors use to counter this situation is by utilizing something called a trailing stop. A trailing stop is a level that is your exit point placed a certain distance behind your trade position. This way, as long as your trade continues to move in your predicted direction, you can have the open position remain to collect more profits. If there was to be a retracement in the direction of the market price, your trailing stop would simply exit your trade at that specified level. You get to protect your account from facing large losses and you locked in the accumulated profits from the trade. It's a double-win for you.

Step 7: Manage your risk

The final step towards trading in the commodity market is to manage your risk in each trade. Chapter 4 of this book discussed many of the risks that you will face trading in this market. But what are some other ways to protect your risk exposure?

Small things that you can do to manage your risk include:

- Keep your losses small compared to your profits.

- If you have a small account, invest a small percentage of it in each trade.

- Don't overtrade the markets.

- Pay attention to the news. This is an important note to remember because it can foreshadow the future price movements that technical analysis can't predict.

- Always be realistic of your trading goals. Don't try to be a millionaire in one night.

- Small, consistent profits will always beat large, random profits.

- Create a trading plan before you enter the commodities market.

- Cut your losses short. Accept that there will be some losses.

- Appreciate each profit that you make.

As long as you follow these small suggestions, you'll significantly minimize the risk exposure that you have from trading in the commodities futures markets.

Chapter 7: Real World Aspects – Applying Your Knowledge in Commodity Futures

As a novice learning all about trading commodities, you'll encounter many systems that promise large profits if you follow their strategies. As enticing as they may be, walk with caution and take the information that is offered with a grain of salt.

The hard truth about commodity trading is that a large percentage of people that will lose their money. In fact, this percentage ranges between 90% - 95%. This doesn't mean that you should give up on trading in this market. Learning the mistakes that 95% are doing to make them lose will help you improve your chances of earning money drastically.

In the marketing world, there are a small number of commodity traders that invest in this market for a living. The one reason why they are able to be successful in this near-impossible market is because they don't treat it as a hobby. They treat it as a business. They also have a plan that they use to monitor each trade that they make. Each trade that they place involves the use of multiple ideas that they've obtained from years of materials that they learned as well as from the years of experience.

The professional trader understands that trading isn't always fun. They have eliminated most of the emotions that may interfere with their trading decisions. Trading properly isn't fun because the strategy that you've polished and developed requires that you remove all emotions in advance.

There are also two different psychological characteristics that divide the winners from the losers: Patience and Discipline.

Having the patience to wait for the right market conditions as well as maintaining the discipline to follow the trading plan religiously will help you mimic the professional traders and stay ahead of the game. It's easier said than done, but when you have your real money on the line, making mistakes is not an option. Trading commodity futures is an emotional daunting task. If you are really determined to be successful in this market, then it will take some hard work and diligence to develop the winning plan.

The time that it will take to fully master the craft of commodities trading will only depend on how much dedication that you put into it. It isn't a market that will give you large profits in a short time span. It's best to follow the guidelines in this book at a steady pace. Take your time with each chapter until you've understood most of the material. Afterwards you can continue to learn more about other advanced subjects that are relevant to trading commodities. It's a growing process and continuously taking one step at a time will help you be more successful as commodity futures investor. Treat this method of trading in a serious manner and you'll begin to see your results sooner than you expect.

Chapter 8: A Final Chapter Insert on Bitcoin and Virtual Currencies, and Some Risks Involved

What is a Virtual Currency?

Although precise definitions offered by others are varied, an IRS definition provides us with a general idea:

> • "Virtual currency is a digital representation of value that functions as a medium of exchange, a unit of account, and/or a store of value.
>
> • In some environments, it operates like 'real' currency, but it does not have legal tender status [in the U.S.].
>
> • Virtual currency that has an equivalent value in real currency, or that acts as a substitute for real currency, is referred to as 'convertible' virtual currency. Bitcoin

is one example of a convertible virtual currency.

• Bitcoin can be digitally traded between users and can be purchased for, or exchanged into, U.S. dollars, Euros, and other real or virtual currencies."

Further, note that one prominent type of virtual currency is cryptocurrency. Cryptocurrency has been described as "an electronic payment system based on cryptographic proof instead of trust, allowing any two willing parties to transact directly with each other without the need for a trusted third party." Satoshi Nakamoto, Bitcoin: A Peer-to-Peer Electronic Cash System (Oct. 31, 2008), available at https://bitcoin.org/bitcoin.pdf (The whitepaper released by Bitcoin's creator)

Risks Buying Virtual Currencies

Purchasing virtual currencies on the cash market comes with a number of risks, including:

• Most cash markets are not regulated or supervised by a government agency.

• Trading platforms may lack customer protections or safeguards against market manipulation.

- Extreme price volatility or "flash" crashes.

- Platforms selling from their own accounts and putting customers at a disadvantage.

What is Bitcoin? Is it a commodity?

Bitcoin is a convertible virtual currency. Yes, virtual currencies, such as Bitcoin, have been determined to be commodities under the Commodity Exchange Act (CEA). While its regulatory oversight authority over commodity cash markets is limited, the U.S. Commodity Futures Trading Commission (CFTC) maintains general anti-fraud and manipulation enforcement authority over virtual currency cash markets as a commodity in interstate commerce.

Bitcoin is currently the largest convertible virtual currency by market capitalization (close to $72 billion in August 2017) Bitcoin was created in 2008 by a person or group that used the name "Satoshi Nakamoto," with the belief that:

> "[w]hat is needed is an electronic payment system based on cryptographic proof instead of trust, allowing any two willing parties to transact directly with each other without the need for a trusted third party."

Bitcoin is "pseudonymous" (or partially anonymous) in that an individual is identified by an alpha-numeric public key/address; it relies on cryptography (and unique digital signatures) for security based on public and private keys and complex mathematical algorithms. Bitcoin runs on a decentralized peer-to-peer network of computers and "miners" that operate on open-source software and do "work" to validate and irrevocably log transactions on a permanent public distributed ledger visible to the entire network. One advantage Bitcoin brought to the scene was that it solves the lack of trust between participants who may be strangers to each other on a public ledger through the transaction validation work noted in the sub-bullet above; and enables the transfer of ownership without the need for a trusted, central intermediary.

What is the Difference between Public and Private Ledger Systems?

Certain virtual currencies operate on public distributed ledger systems that capture "blocks" of transactions – there is no inherent trust in this decentralized system. Virtual currencies create an economic incentive for dispersed, independent, computers, or groups of computers, around the world to confirm transactions and perform verifiable "work" (that creates consensus) to publish a new block of transactions on the public ledger in exchange for a payment of the applicable virtual currency.

Private / permissioned distributed ledger networks typically have some degree of trust between participants. Private ledger systems allow a network of known participants to share transaction information between themselves more efficiently. While cryptography and consensus may still be involved in private ledger systems, these systems do not necessarily involve a virtual currency that may serve as the economic incentive for miner or validator participation in public networks.

Some Sample Potential Use Cases of Virtual Currencies

Store of Value:

• Like precious metals, many virtual currencies are a "non-yielding" asset (meaning they do not pay dividends or interest), but they may be more fungible, divisible, and portable.

• Limited or finite supply of virtual currencies may contrast with 'real' (fiat) currencies.

• Trading in virtual currencies may result in capital gains or losses. Trading in virtual currencies may involve significant speculation and volatility risk (see Virtual Currency Risks section below).

Payments and Transactions:

- Some merchants and online stores are accepting virtual currencies in exchange for physical and digital goods (i.e., payments).

- Some public blockchain systems rely on the payment of fees in virtual currency form in order to power the network and underlying transactions.

Transfer / Move Money:

- Domestic and international money transfer (e.g., remittances) in order to increase efficiencies and potentially reduce related fees.

Blockchain, or distributed ledger technology, underpins many virtual currencies, but can also be used within private, permissioned ledger systems – versions of public and private systems may be used by: Financial Institutions, Trading & Payment Platforms, Governments, and Cross-Industry Entities. Governments could utilize the blockchain for General Records Management, Title & Ownership Records Management (e.g., real property deeds and title transfer), and Regulatory Reporting and Oversight. The major Cross-Industry applications could be Smart

Contracts (i.e., self-executing agreements), Resource / Asset Sharing Agreements (e.g., allowing rental of a personal car left behind during a vacation or allowing rental of excess computer or data storage.

Virtual Currencies are Commodities

The definition of "commodity" in the CEA is broad; it can mean a physical commodity, such as an agricultural product (e.g., wheat, cotton) or natural resource (e.g., gold, oil). It can mean a currency or interest rate. The CEA definition of "commodity" also includes "all services, rights, and interests in which contracts for future delivery are presently or in the future dealt in." The CFTC has oversight over futures, options, and derivatives contracts. The CFTC's jurisdiction is implicated when a virtual currency is used in a derivatives contract, or if there is fraud or manipulation involving a virtual currency traded in interstate commerce. Beyond instances of fraud or manipulation, the CFTC generally does not oversee "spot" or cash market exchanges and transactions involving virtual currencies that do not utilize margin, leverage, or financing.

Some Examples of Permitted Activities

- TeraExchange, LLC, a Swap Execution Facility ("SEF") registered with the CFTC, entered in to the virtual currency market in 2014 by listing a Bitcoin swap for trading. Trading on a SEF platform is limited to "eligible contract participants," a type of sophisticated trader, which includes various financial institutions and persons, with assets above specified statutory minimums.

- North American Derivatives Exchange Inc. ("NADEX"), a designated contract market ("DCM"), listed binary options based on the Tera Bitcoin Price Index from November 2014 to December 2016. Retail customers may trade on NADEX.

- LedgerX, LLC ("LedgerX") registered with the CFTC as a SEF and Derivative Clearing Organization ("DCO") in July 2017. It plans to list digital currency options.

Some Examples of Some Prohibited Activities

- Price manipulation of a virtual currency traded in interstate commerce.

- Pre-arranged or wash trading in an exchange-traded virtual currency swap or futures contract.

- A virtual currency futures or option contract or swap traded on a domestic platform or facility that has not registered with the CFTC as a SEF or DCM.

- Certain schemes involving virtual currency marketed to retail customers, such as off-exchange financed commodity transactions with persons who fail to register with the CFTC.

ICOs, Virtual Tokens, and CFTC Oversight

The Securities and Exchange Commission ("SEC") recently released a report about an Initial Coin Offering or "ICO" (the "DAO Report"). The DAO Report explains that "The DAO" is an example of a "Decentralized Autonomous Organization," which is a "virtual" organization embodied in computer code and executed on a distributed ledger or blockchain. Investors exchanged Ether, a virtual currency, for virtual DAO "Tokens" to fund projects in which the investors would share in anticipated earnings. DAO Tokens could be resold on web-based platforms. Based on the facts and circumstances, the SEC determined that DAO Tokens are "securities" under the federal securities laws. There is no inconsistency between the SEC's analysis and the CFTC's determination that virtual currencies are commodities and that virtual tokens may be commodities or derivatives contracts depending on the particular facts and circumstances. The CFTC looks beyond form and considers the actual substance and purpose of an activity when applying the federal commodities laws and CFTC regulations

Risks of Virtual Currencies

While virtual currencies have potential benefits, this emerging space also involves various risks, including:

- Operational Risks

- Cybersecurity Risks

- Speculative Risks

- Fraud and Manipulation Risks

Virtual currencies are relatively unproven and may not perform as expected (for example, some have questioned whether public distributed ledgers are in fact immutable). Investors and users of virtual currencies should educate themselves about these and other risks before getting involved.

• ***Virtual Currency: Operational Risk***

Conduct extensive research before giving any money or personal information to a virtual currency platform. The virtual currency marketplace is comprised of many different platforms where you can convert one type of virtual currency into another or into real currency, if offered. Many of these platforms are not subject to the supervision which applies to regulated exchanges. For example, if they engage in only certain spot or cash market transactions and do not utilize margin, leverage, or financing, they may be subject to federal and state money transmission and anti-money laundering laws, but they do not have to follow all the rules that regulated exchanges operate under. Some virtual currency platforms may be missing critical system safeguards and customer protection related systems; without adequate safeguards, customers may lose some or all of their virtual assets.

• ***Virtual Currency: Cybersecurity Risk***

Keep your property in safe accounts and carefully verify digital wallet addresses. Some platforms may "commingle" (mix) customer assets in shared accounts (at a bank for real currency or a digital wallet for virtual currency). This may affect whether or how you can withdraw your currency. Depending on the structure and security of the digital wallet, some may be vulnerable to hacks, resulting in the theft of virtual currency or loss of customer assets. If a bad actor gains access to your private key, it can take your virtual currency with limited or no recourse. When transferring virtual currency, be sure to confirm the destination wallet address, even when using "copy and paste." It is possible for hackers to change digital wallet addresses on your computer.

- *Virtual Currency: Speculative Risk*

Only invest what you are willing and able to lose! The virtual currency marketplace has been subject to substantial volatility and price swings. An individual or coordinated group trading a large amount of virtual currency at once could affect the price, depending on the overall amount of trading in the marketplace. Periods of high volatility with inadequate trade volume may create adverse market conditions, leading to harmful effects such as customer orders being filled at undesirable prices. Some advertisements promise guaranteed returns – this can be a common tactic with fraudulent schemes.

- *Virtual Currency: Fraud & Manipulation Risk*

Carefully research the platform you want to use, and pay close attention to the fee structure and systems safeguards. Unregistered virtual currency platforms may not be able to adequately protect against market abuses by other traders. For example, recent news articles discuss potential "spoofing" activity and other manipulative behavior that can negatively affect prices. Some virtual currency platforms may be selling you virtual currency directly from their own account – these types of transactions may give the platform unfair advantages and sometimes resemble fraudulent "bucket shop" schemes. There is also a risk of *Ponzi schemers* and fraudsters seeking to capitalize on the current attention focused on virtual currencies.

What is a Ponzi scheme?

A Ponzi scheme is an investment fraud that involves the payment of purported returns to existing investors from funds contributed by new investors. Ponzi scheme organizers often solicit new investors by promising to invest funds in opportunities claimed to generate high returns with little or no risk. In many Ponzi schemes, the fraudsters focus on attracting new money to make promised payments to earlier-stage investors to create the false appearance that investors are profiting from a legitimate business.

Why do Ponzi Schemes Collapse?

With little or no legitimate earnings, Ponzi schemes require a consistent flow of money from new investors to continue. Ponzi schemes tend to collapse when it becomes difficult to recruit new investors or when a large number of investors ask to cash out.

How did Ponzi Schemes get their Name?

The schemes are named after Charles Ponzi, who duped thousands of New England residents into investing in a postage stamp speculation scheme back in the 1920s. At a time when the annual interest rate for bank accounts was five percent, Ponzi promised investors that he could provide a 50% return in just 90 days. Ponzi initially bought a small number of international mail coupons in support of his scheme, but quickly switched to using incoming funds from new investors to pay purported returns to earlier investors.

What are Some Ponzi Scheme "Red Flags"?

Many Ponzi schemes share common characteristics. Look for these warning signs:

High investment returns with little or no risk. Every investment carries some degree of risk, and investments yielding higher returns typically involve more risk. Be highly suspicious of any "guaranteed" investment opportunity.

Overly consistent returns. Investment values tend to go up and down over time, especially those offering potentially high returns. Be suspect of an investment that continues to generate regular, positive returns regardless of overall market conditions.

Unregistered investments. Ponzi schemes typically involve investments that have not been registered with the SEC or with state regulators. Registration is important because it provides investors with access to key information about the company's management, products, services, and finances.

Unlicensed sellers. Federal and state securities laws require investment professionals and their firms to be licensed or registered. Most Ponzi schemes involve unlicensed individuals or unregistered firms.

Secretive and/or complex strategies. Avoiding investments you do not understand, or for which you cannot get complete information, is a good rule of thumb.

Issues with paperwork. Do not accept excuses regarding why you cannot review information about an investment in writing. Also, account statement errors and inconsistencies may be signs that funds are not being invested as promised.

Difficulty receiving payments. Be suspicious if you do not receive a payment or have difficulty cashing out your investment. Keep in mind that Ponzi scheme promoters routinely encourage participants to "roll over" investments and sometimes promise returns offering even higher returns on the amount rolled over.

What Steps Can I Take to Avoid Ponzi Schemes and Other Investment Frauds?

Whether you are a first-time investor or have been investing for many years, there are some basic questions you should always ask before you commit your hard-earned money to an investment.

The SEC sees too many investors who might have avoided trouble and losses if they had asked questions from the start and verified the answers with information from independent sources.

When you consider your next investment opportunity, start with these five questions:

Is the seller licensed?

Is the investment registered?

How do the risks compare with the potential rewards?

Do I understand the investment?

www.ingramcontent.com/pod-product-compliance
Lightning Source LLC
Chambersburg PA
CBHW072206170526
45158CB00004BB/1779